www.finishinglinepress.com

ON A ROAD

poems by

Jeffrey Kingman

Finishing Line Press
Georgetown, Kentucky

ON A ROAD

ACKNOWLEDGMENTS

"Stopover" was published in *Sparkle + Blink* No. 99, 2019, as part of their
Quiet Lightning reading series.

Thank you to the Pom-Poms group (Sheila Sumner, Caroline Kessler,
Andrew Taw) and to Jessica Moll and Gretchen Stengel for their
encouragement and support.

Thank you to Krystal Hipps for the cover and to Finishing Line Press for
publishing my book. Hats off to FLP and all small presses for the important
work they do.

Very special thanks to Rusty Morrison for helping me clear the way toward
writing this book.

Publisher: Leah Maines
Editor: Christen Kincaid
Cover Art: OpenSFHistory / wnp36.04306.jpg
Author Photo: S.N. Jacobson
Cover Design: Krystal Hipps

Printed in the USA on acid-free paper.
Order online: www.finishinglinepress.com
also available on amazon.com

Author inquiries and mail orders:
Finishing Line Press
P. O. Box 1626
Georgetown, Kentucky 40324
U. S. A.

Table of Contents

after Jack Kerouac

Sharp for Any Kind

first time in my life

sawdust   railroad hats there weren't even any lights

in a minute

all I did was

yell back we relaxed
                    a flag
                    dynamite

tail lights   blinked   saw a pretty girl

roaring tires

in a minute

Men Along the Country

what's a farm
they fish wool

a blond hand
            sneaked the platform

    his goal to bounce

  somebody passed the bottom of it
was there room

        a young city boy
        worried lips wet from thinking

        shoes for a journey
        why life wasn't interesting

        why language tall old and black with soot
        so far you couldn't see

    let me off

Easy Boy

now and then a big truck
empty sandbags blew
the horizon blank

except for a tree
sound surrounded me   zoom
stepped over the broken potato chip
understood

I stopped marching after lunch but
never could remember
so marched right along
                                    falling

falling over
put your arms out
still I could drown
I loved that tree what else

the last truck came
they wanted my sandwiches
I said no

Off I Went

soda fountain Egypt
a brief rancher

                  Nebraska I ain't he said

or that's what he meant

                but got sleepy

his aunt-a-penny
    couldn't figure out how his name

                got writ on the water tank

the poor aunt said a thin drizzle of rain sounded like Europe

             I didn't know him under an elm

      where you at
he said

                  I didn't know

        near a big gas station
                I was told

town had a nice soda fountain
                pie and ice cream

Watch Them Disappear

moths in the darkness
they had no cigarettes

fallen absurd to proud devices
leaning out of their trance didn't work

a sweet song flat over the boulevard
no I don't   but he loved the way she said it

tender ear
ain't no flowers

they never asked
I kept offering

he lost her out by the towering red radio
said he felt cold as a babe in a strange coverlet

I zoomed through   squandering gracious

All Floors Are the Same

stuck my head out

like hell into the local museum
paws wandered through

floors are all the same

deeds in hiding pretty
sullen

eight o'clock in the morning
shacks give me a headache

all I wanted to do was my mind

reckon a mail box tottering headdress
golden flare incessant

cloud museum a shack

all I wanted to do
careening

Drink Drank

boyhood sisters from bottles
after the great northern kitchenette carpeted stairs narrow
negative smile points at a hand
arty America

      mother's housework swank dinner
      greatest poet six in the morning surrounded by very little
                                        a stain from the East

                broken half-blood whisky drop

        a helluva harbinger plants green greens
        marbles in the study slide the coldcut platter

rolltop dust

      the madman points at his hand
      making the department store make
      the poolhall make
      the mountain

With One Thread

loll that grassy old church

where we sing
            except in the ravine

by the count of ten harvests move north

such a together   my ticket to halfway

vague plans to meet
wish each other
as soon as frightened five minutes
kiss the storied river
or me

nine yawning ninety

toiling sleeping
            walk in the fizzle

born in sprinklers the hot sun forget that car driving away sound

hand me up the brass rail

Not a Bit

       found alone with no shirt
took off stranger absolute
    a man in hurrying trouble disagreed
         something made   a rawness oozed
could've shaped it into a

    shape

        the streets fallen out

no money

    gossip a party took place

       in an alley

three girls the same

    who's a stranger   the one for me

       is the one for me

Get Clean

grab your ghost and polish

covered in an inch
a porch a well

all we had
to do was clean it out

groaning mournful opera
luckily the rush of other things

a wonderful nightmare

razors
hairbrushes cologne

girls who went
mostly young kids

dancing to nothing

kiss them disheveled
laden into buckets

ushers excitement   you could marry the litmus

a come-on
hollowing happy

Fixed Price

dawning for dimes
        on a pinned note in a canyon

I don't know if he ever finished supper

wife is together
        why her *thems* always tie to a point
        because isn't her French English

     she calls Paradise paradise

hollering at him
        from up the ridge

        they only gave me half

haggle

      waitresses

I slept in a cot by the window

      shovel mouth
      good appetite

Hollywood Treatment

bored and hated us
rainy hours scribbling
current of steep streaming cars
the Greyhound a bare explanation over the side

gloom job intimate
it was the bastards had stories

noisy characters in westerns
always disappointed by funny hearts

or navy ships blasting

the time had come to pull the anchor myself   rust
but some silly remark some door in the face
now was not the time
when oars float

then I climbed another hill and there were the horses

sharp dresser have a drink kid
I went around to all the fish as anybody else

pretty soon pretty soon

she was bored and hated us

pretty soon pretty

soon

Bad Proportions

a hum in a hotel

    far
        across
the same way I'd come in

    melon fields pressed grapes
bag of peanuts on the bench

  so I stayed another day

  my last
      red
        sun

    I turned snapped my head
gone the skinny guy with curly hair
brokendown rooster   beard and sandals

    I panicked
rushed off to the farthest highest cliff
the horrid Susquehanna rushing below
a number in relation to a whole

Hold Tight

she went out in the mud to find a head between his knees

the two foggy bundles wandered there together

from the steps of the motel court

alone mixing up their boys   a prowl car came by

possessions moved along self-propelled   hunchbacks

a penny pile outside the arcade

their remaining money dissipates   a different kind of fog

the kind that blows out your mouth

his mouth her mouth

a mouth

brushed the sand off the sheets

three or four sevens in his pocket

she sat down to make him look right off his truck

yanked at each other in the clutch

a new idea they talked a little fool

Denver Bakersfield Sabinal Fresno

fruit stands hundred rickety trucks

                    drinkyard railroad
                    a crate and a fire

we rounded up a little boy

she came waving at me across the street

                    I knew nothing
                    about not knowing

                    the cheapest one was vacant
                    stove and a cracked mirror

a sad sooty red

                    when we woke
                    it was the next fifteen days

                    ran between the vineyards
                    truck broke down

we found a place where we could find a place

                    but couldn't go
                    from all the spinning

the family shack got dark our faces inside

light poured out the door

                    the old man warned me
                    only three dollars per three dollars

now I could get there and go off

        off a ways away
        off off awe full

not for my baby and the baby

I'm past everyone four hundred miles south

        the bulk of a continent far across
        the same way I'd come in
        throwing up all the names

I Was Asleep at the Time

stood under a streetlamp and thumb

then off to plod along in the teeth of traffic

if hit he'd go flying

windshield covered with a sheen of ice

plumbing fixtures around Pennsylvania

motel office years and years

shouts and arguments and yodeling

drive a head out the window

if this kept up passengers down the mountainside

farmer offered to help a nearsighted girl peering into the snow

getting much colder at night

Three Days and Three Nights

made it there in ten hours
it was dusk millions and millions
figure the losses
now it was too late
        had his own life
thought they were going to stick
the girl herself on the phone
        wanted to know how everything happened
and all the time every moment
pitched our long arms
        into the beginning with socks sticking out
a hundred drugstore phonebooths the girl herself
wouldn't say anything refused to commit
we'd pick her up on the way
        through the tunnel into New Jersey
two hours later
Groucho Marx couldn't eat so well
how we were poor
rattling the window pane

See To It the Bell Doesn't Ring

you know when everything is decided
                        the whole idea

but how should I know what's on everybody's mind

I went home to rest
        pants dresses thrown around   a great forum

this ain't a hotel
            or a washed-out bottom of a barrel

said goodbye and promised
                a big long look out the window

insisted on steering
        lurking to make you start and see

pulled off to find some sad crazy
                        I'd soon find out

hustling for bread somewhere in town
                        wallet of Christ

if you're poor you have to listen when they tell you

Stopover

        snored up to eighty

snuck

                through the gas station

     wheels linger now

what's regular   ordinary

the air

         so sweet at dusk

    we stare ahead

    at the stop

           sitstill

      she doesn't know what to say

goes right on reading as if words are the wilderness

Notes

Each of these poems contains words and phrases borrowed from Kerouac's *On the Road*. Many phrases are changed according to my creative needs. Phrases that are quoted exactly (or nearly exactly) are noted below.

Sharp for Any Kind
Part One, Chapter 3: "sharp for any kind" "in a minute"

Watch Them Disappear
Part One, Chapter 4: "they had no cigarettes" "they never asked" "I kept offering"

Get Clean
Part One, Chapter 9: "all we had to do was clean it out"

Fixed Price
Part One, Chapter 11: "I slept in a cot by the window"

Hollywood Treatment
Part One, Chapter 11: "then I climbed another hill and there were the" "she was bored and hated us"

Bad Proportions
Part One, Chapter 11: "so I stayed another day"

Hold Tight
Part One, Chapter 13: "brushed the sand off the sheets"

Denver Bakersfield Sabinal Fresno
Part One, Chapter 13: "the cheapest one was vacant" "sad and sooty red" "light poured out the door"

I Was Asleep at the Time
Part One, Chapter 13: "I was asleep at the time"
Part One, Chapter 14: "plumbing fixtures around Pennsylvania" "in the teeth of … traffic"

Three Days and Three Nights
Part Two, Chapter 3: "made it there in ten hours" "socks sticking out" "refused to commit"

See To It the Bell Doesn't Ring
Part Two, Chapter 6: "saw to it the bell didn't ring" "hustling for bread somewhere in town"
Part Two, Chapter 5: "pants, dresses thrown around"

Jeffrey Kingman lives by the Napa River in Vallejo, California. He has written several books, including a full-length poetry book, *Beyond That Hill I Gather*, which contains portrait poems of notable women. It won the 2018 Eyelands Book Award (Greece) for an unpublished poetry book. He also wrote a young adult novel, *Moto Girl* (unpublished), about a 12-year-old girl learning to ride motocross.

Jeff is the winner of the 2012 *Revolution House* Flash Fiction Contest, and the winner of the Red Berry Editions 2015 Broadside Contest. He has been a finalist in many contests including the 2018 Hillary Gravendyk Prize poetry book competition, the 2015 Blue Light Press Chapbook Competition, the 2014 Sow's Ear Poetry Competition, and the 2013 Frost Place Chapbook Fellowship. He has been published in *PANK, Crack the Spine, Squaw Valley Review, The Offbeat, Sparkle & Blink, lo-ball, Off Channel, Grey Sparrow, decomP, North Atlantic Review, Picaroon Poetry,* and others.

Jeff has a Master's degree in Music Composition and has played drums in rock bands most of his life.